Step-by-Step
Origami

D1549261

Clive Stevens

Search Press

First published in Great Britain 2002

Search Press Limited
Wellwood, North Farm Road,
Tunbridge Wells, Kent TN2 3DR

Reprinted 2004 (twice), 2005

ISBN 1 90397 535 2

Suppliers
If you have difficulty in obtaining any of the materials
and equipment mentioned in this book, then please visit
the Search Press website for details of suppliers:
www.searchpress.com

Alternatively, you can write to the Publishers at the
address above, for a current list of stockists, which
includes firms who operate a mail-order service.

Acknowledgements

Printed in China by WKT Company Ltd

To my dear Sue for her endless patience, and to Sarah and Tom who I know will enjoy these projects.

Special thanks to G F Smith & Son
London Ltd, 2 Leathermarket,
Weston Street, London SE1 3ET for
supplying the paper used in this
book. Many thanks are also due to
everyone at Search Press who helped
me with this book, especially
Editorial Director Roz Dace,
Editor Sophie Kersey and
Designer Juan Hayward.

The Publishers would like to say a
huge thank you to Jessika Kwan,
Ellie Hayward,
Joy Jones Odeh,
Edwin Clifford-Coupe,
Mushed Miah, Coral Godden,
Jordan Thomas, Hannah Sharma and
Ryan Hills.

Finally, special thanks to
Southborough Primary School,
Tunbridge Wells.

Contents

Introduction

It is generally believed that paper was invented in China around the first century AD, and the Chinese soon began to fold the new material into decorative shapes. When paper was introduced to Japan in the sixth century AD by Buddhist monks, it rapidly became an important part of their culture. Paper was used as part of many religious ceremonies, and even as a building material. It was the Japanese who turned paper folding into an art, which in Japan is as important as painting and sculpture. Origami comes from the Japanese words for folding, *ori*, and paper, *kami*.

The Japanese passed on their paper folding designs by word of mouth; many were passed down from mother to daughter. In the early days, paper was too expensive to be used for fun, so paper folding was done only for important ceremonies. Paper butterflies were made to decorate the cups for *sake* (rice wine) used at Japanese weddings.

By the seventeenth century, paper had become less expensive, and origami had become a popular pastime in Japan. The first origami books with diagrams and instructions were published in the early eighteenth century.

Today, master paper folders can be found all over the world. Folding techniques have improved so much that they would have astounded the ancient Japanese who invented origami.

In this book, you will learn how to make good, crisp folds so that your paper will hold the right shapes. Follow the instructions carefully, and this is all you need to know to make some simple but very effective projects.

In origami, many different shapes can be made from a few simple bases. The Origami Bases chapter on pages 10–11 shows you how to make two of these bases, and once you have mastered folding these, you are ready to make some very impressive projects!

Don't worry if your folding doesn't work the first time. Go over the instructions and pictures again carefully, and you will soon find where you went wrong.

You hardly need any materials to do origami, and it is easy to become hooked. After a few tries, you will learn the folds off by heart, and then all you need is a piece of paper to produce impressive designs that will amaze your friends!

Opposite
This amazing origami beetle is only about 2.5cm (1in) long. It was designed and folded by the Italian paper folder, Alfredo Giunta.

Designed and folded by Alfredo Giunta. Photograph by Robin Macey.

Materials

Origami is the best known of all the paper crafts. The rules of origami do not allow paper cutting, gluing or decoration of the paper – it may only be folded. For this reason, very little equipment is required.

Paper is the most important thing to start with! When practising origami, I use simple white paper that is made for computer printers. This is very cheap to buy in large amounts, and can be used for most origami designs. However, for the projects in this book, coloured paper will look most effective.

You can use **paper** of many different types, colours and thicknesses for origami. You can also use **thin card**. **Patterned papers** such as **wrapping paper** are ideal for some projects. **Origami paper** can be bought in craft shops. It comes in packs containing various different sizes, and is usually coloured one side and white on the other. It is thinner than standard printer paper and a little stronger. It is best for two-tone models such as the Paper Penguin project on pages 16–17. **Metallic paper**s can be very effective for projects such as the Space Rocket on pages 26–27. They are metallic on one side and white on the other, and can be bought from art and craft shops.

A **long ruler** is useful for measuring paper before cutting it to the right size.

Scissors are used only for cutting paper to size. No paper cutting is allowed in origami once the shape is folded.

An **ordinary ruler** can be used to create a fold, as in the Paper Penguin project on pages 16–17.

A **pencil** or a **cocktail stick** are used to curl the edges of paper for a finishing touch, as in the Folded Flower project on pages 24–25.

For some projects such as the Obi Bookmark on pages 22–23, you will need to cut strips out of **large pieces of paper**. These are A2 size.

Techniques

Folding in half

1 Fold the bottom corners upwards to meet the top corners. This will make a horizontal fold.

2 Make a crease in the middle. Press with your finger from the middle to the edge, then from the middle to the other edge. Make sure the corners stay together.

3 Reinforce the crease by pressing it with your fingernail.

Folding diagonally

Start with a square piece of paper. Lift up one corner and meet it up with the corner diagonally opposite to it. Make a crease in the middle of the paper and work out from the middle to the sides. This makes a diagonal fold.

Folding at an angle

Lay a strip of paper horizontally. Fold part of the strip downwards so that the edges of the strip make a right angle, like the corner of a square.

Reverse Folding (internal)

Reverse folding means that you push a fold until it folds in the opposite direction. A valley fold (which dips downwards) becomes a mountain fold (which points upwards), and vice versa. This internal reverse fold is used for the Flapping Bird project on pages 28–29.

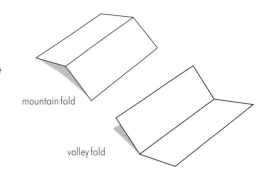

mountain fold

valley fold

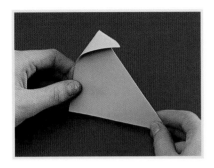

1 Fold a square piece of paper in half diagonally. Fold the top corner down as shown and crease it sharply.

2 Open the paper up slightly. Pull the top point towards you. Reverse the mountain fold in the middle of the point, making it a valley fold.

3 Remake the diagonal fold and open it up to show the point with its valley fold.

Reverse Folding (external)

This type of external reverse fold is used for the Paper Penguin project on pages 16–17.

1 Take a square piece of paper and fold it diagonally. Fold down the top point as shown and crease firmly.

2 Open up with the diagonal mountain fold facing towards you. Fold the top point towards you. Reverse the fold in the middle of the point. Now remake the diagonal fold, so that the point comes down on the outside of the diagonal fold.

Origami Bases

Many origami designs come from a few simple bases. Here are two bases which can lead to all sorts of different projects.

Bird Base

This base is used to make the Flapping Bird project on page 28. Steps 1 to 3 also start off the Folded Flower project on page 24.

1 Take a square of paper. Fold the square diagonally. Crease it firmly and open. Fold on the other diagonal, crease and open. Turn the paper over so that your diagonal folds are mountain folds, as shown above.

2 Now fold up the bottom two corners to meet the top two corners and fold the paper in half horizontally. Crease, unfold, and then fold in half the other way to make a cross shape. Turn the paper over and place it as shown, so that the horizontal folds are mountain folds, and the diagonal folds are valley folds that dip down.

3

Hold the edges of a horizontal fold as shown. Move your hands in together until the paper forms a square. There should be two flaps on either side of the square as shown.

open end

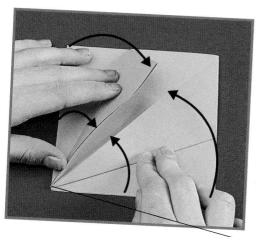

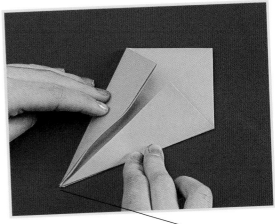

open end

open end

 4 Fold the front flaps, bringing the edges in to the middle. Make sure the open end of the shape is at the bottom as shown.

5 Turn over and repeat on the other side.

Rocket Base

This is used in the Space Rocket project on pages 26–27 and the Blow-up Box on pages 30–31.

 1

Start making the Bird Base, but only go as far as Step 2. Turn the paper over so that the diagonal folds are mountain folds and the horizontal folds are valley folds. Fold one of the diagonal folds and hold it by the corners. Push your hands downwards to form a triangle.

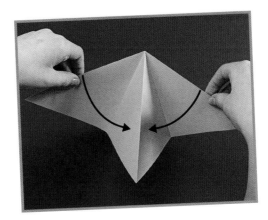

2

The triangle should have two flaps on either side, like the square made in step 3 of the Bird Base.

Note If your origami bases have not turned out right, check these things:
• Make sure your folds are sharply creased.
• If your diagonal folds are mountain folds, your horizontal folds should be valley folds.
• Make sure the open end of the shape is at the bottom.

11

Layered Fan

Many people have learnt to make a simple fan by folding a piece of paper into a concertina shape. This may have been your first introduction to paper folding! However, folding this way can lead to uneven folds and an untidy finished fan. This is an origami fan, made from basic valley and mountain folds. This method means that you fold the paper so that it is divided equally.

YOU WILL NEED
Three different coloured papers:
10 x 30cm (4 x 11¾in)
12 x 30cm (4¾ x 11¾in)
14 x 30cm (5½ x 11¾in)

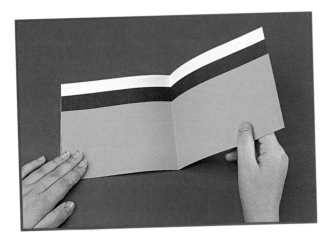

1 Place all three pieces of paper together as shown. Fold them in half and unfold.

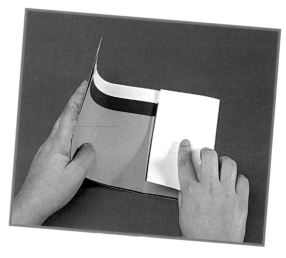

2 Fold the right and left edges in to the centre line.

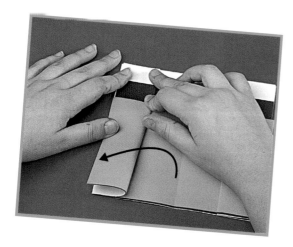

3 Take one of the edges that you have folded in to the middle, and fold it back to the new edge. Repeat the other side as shown.

4 Fold in half, bringing the double outside edges together.

5 Fold the top flap back. Turn the paper over and repeat on the other side.

6 Open up and pinch at the bottom to form a multicoloured fan.

FURTHER IDEAS

Make fans from patterned origami paper, wrapping paper, or even beautiful Japanese handmade papers.

Secrets Folder

This handy folder is made using simple folds and also a tuck fold. It can be any size you want, from a tiny purse for loose change, to a folder like the one shown here, for larger secrets! Remember that the folder you end up with will be much smaller than the piece of paper you start with. You need to cut down an A2 size piece of paper to make a folder as big as the one shown in these photographs. What you hide in your secrets folder is up to you!

YOU WILL NEED
Coloured or patterned paper
30 x 50cm (12 x 20in)

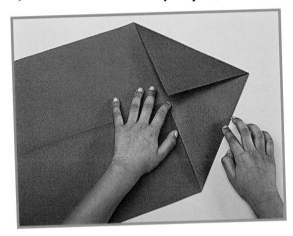

1 Place the paper, shiny side down and fold in half horizontally. Unfold. Fold the two top corners in to the centre line.

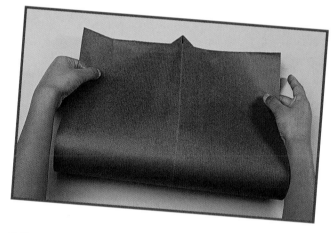

2 Fold the bottom edge up to the point at the top.

3 Now fold the outside edges in to the centre fold.

Fold the bottom edge to the top of the diagonal folds.

Tuck the flap into the front pocket.

Fold the point down to form the front flap of the secrets folder.

FURTHER IDEAS

Try using metallic or patterned papers, or decorate a piece of paper yourself using paints or felt tip pens before folding.

Paper Penguin

Origami paper with black on one side and white on the other works perfectly for this project. Using very few folds, you can create something that stands up like a real penguin. Penguins are some of the most sociable of all birds – they like to swim and feed in groups, so why not make a whole group of penguins and a paper pool for them to go fishing in?

YOU WILL NEED
One 10cm (4in) square piece of paper, black on one side and white on the other.

1 Take your square piece of paper. Fold it diagonally in half with the white on the inside to make a crease, then unfold. Turn the paper over. Take a corner at one end of the diagonal fold, and fold it up 2½cm (1in) as shown. Crease sharply.

2 Reverse the diagonal fold so that the white is on the outside, to make the shape shown.

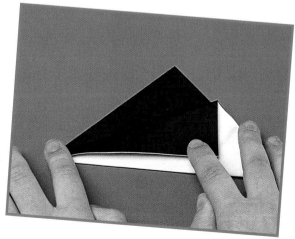

3 Fold the top point down to 1½cm (½in) from the bottom fold, and crease. Turn the paper over and repeat. This step is like making the wings on a paper aeroplane.

Place a ruler over the shape and fold the point down against the edge of a ruler at the angle shown. Remove the ruler and crease.

5

Open up slightly and pull the point towards you, making an external reverse fold as shown on page 9. This will make the penguin's head point downwards.

6

Crease the penguin again so that it is completely flat and open it up to reveal the finished penguin.

FURTHER IDEAS
Make a group of penguins in different colours and sizes, and maybe a paper pool for them to dive into!

Picture Frame

This simple origami frame is the perfect place to put one of your drawings, or a favourite photograph. Use thin card instead of paper, as this will make a stronger frame. The picture that goes inside this frame can be up to 14.5cm (5¾in) square, but don't forget that only a 10.5cm (4in) square in the middle will show.

1 Fold the square diagonally corner to corner.

2 Open up and repeat on the other two corners.

3 Open up again. Your diagonal folds should be valley folds. Fold one corner down to the centre. Fold the other corners down to the centre.

4 Turn the paper over and again fold all corners down to the centre.

5 Turn the base over and fold all the points out to their corners.

6 Measure your picture frame. Draw a picture or find a photograph this size, remembering that the corners will be hidden by the frame. Slide the picture into the frame.

FURTHER IDEAS
Fold only as far as step 4 to make a drinks mat. Cover the mat in plastic to make it spill-proof.

Japanese Card

People have been sending one another greetings cards for hundreds of years. The first ones celebrated holidays or religious festivals, but nowadays they are sent for all kinds of reasons. Handmade cards are even more special than shop-bought ones. This Japanese greetings card has contrasting shades of the same colour to make it eye-catching. You open the flaps and write your message inside.

YOU WILL NEED
Two pieces of contrasting coloured paper, 23.5cm (9in) square

1 Put the squares of paper one on top of the other. Measure across the diagonal and mark it in to thirds of 11cm (4¼in) each.

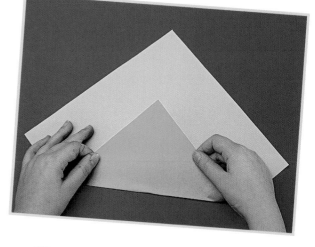

2 Fold the corner along the diagonal. Fold on your first mark, up to your second mark.

3 Unfold. Turn the paper round and fold the opposite corner up to your first fold.

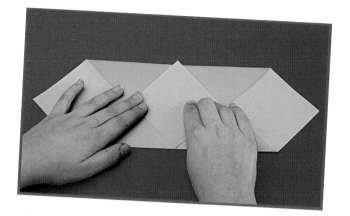

Fold one corner up to the top edge. Take the opposite corner out from under the top flap and fold it down to the bottom edge.

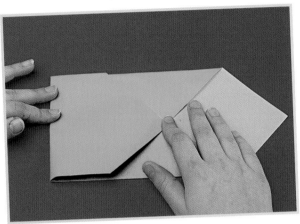

5

Fold one side in to cover the central light-coloured square. Fold the other side in as well.

6 Fold the triangular flap out to the outside edge and repeat the other side.

FURTHER IDEAS

Create a traditional Japanese card from glossy black and red paper.

Obi Bookmark

This traditional folding technique looks like the sash or *obi* worn round a Japanese kimono. Use bright, contrasting colours to give your bookmark a modern look. You need long strips of paper to start with, so make sure you cut them from an A2 size sheet. Once you have mastered the overlapping technique, you will be able to make a variety of bookmarks in different lengths and colours. They make the ideal gift for a friend who likes reading.

YOU WILL NEED
Two strips of paper in contrasting colours, 54 x 3cm (21¼ x 1¼in)
Scissors
Ruler

26cm (10¼in) from left

1 Put one strip on top of the other. Fold the strips at an angle, as shown on page 8. The fold should come 26cm (10¼in) from the left-hand end of the strips.

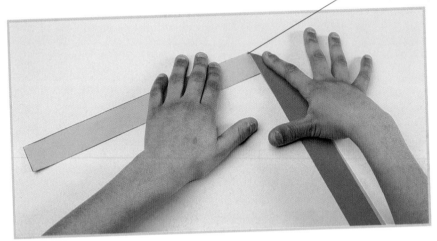

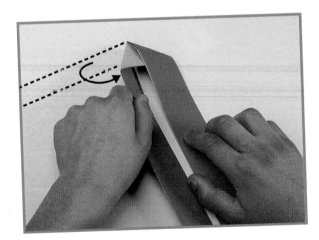

2 Fold the left-hand strips under at an angle. The strips should run parallel with the right-hand strips.

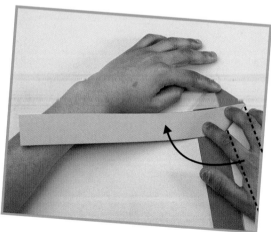

3 Fold the right-hand strip at an angle as shown.

Slip the top right-hand strips under the left-hand strips.

Repeat steps 2, 3 and 4. Carry on doing this until four squares have been formed.

Fold the excess under neatly or trim the ends using scissors.

FURTHER IDEAS

Use contrasting papers: weave textured and glossy paper or patterned and plain paper together.

Folded Flower

This origami flower starts out as a square, but with a few folds it turns in to a flower shape, and curling the ends of the petals gives it a natural beauty. Why not make lots of flowers in different colours, with straws or pipe cleaners for stems. Then you can arrange them in a vase or bouquet.

1 Fold the square diagonally. Crease it firmly and open up. Then fold it on the other diagonal and open up the paper as shown above. Your diagonal folds should be mountain folds.

2 Fold up the bottom two corners to meet the top two corners and make a horizontal fold. Crease, unfold and then fold the paper in half the other way. Now your horizontal folds are mountain folds and your diagonal folds are valley folds.

3 Hold the ends of a horizontal fold with both hands as shown, moving your hands together until the paper forms a square with two flaps on each side.

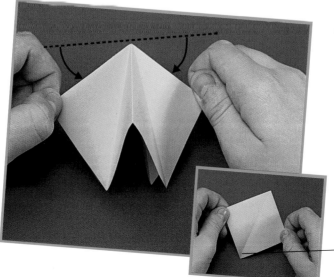

open end

24

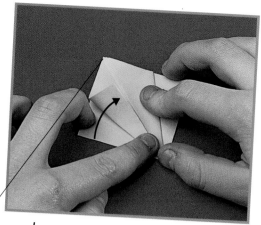

open end

4 Turn the square the other way up so that the open point is at the top. Fold the front flaps as shown, bringing the edges into the middle. Crease firmly. Turn over and repeat on the other side.

open end

5

Unfold one of the small flaps and reverse the fold so that it becomes a valley fold instead of a mountain fold. Repeat with the other three flaps.

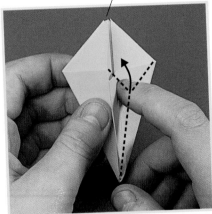

6 Open out the flower. Using a pencil or a cocktail stick, roll the tops of all four points down to create the natural curl of a petal.

FURTHER IDEAS
Make much bigger flowers, and then make smaller flowers without curling the petals. These make centres for the big flowers.

Space Rocket

This rocket is made from silver metallic origami paper that is white on the other side. It has legs that point outwards at an angle, so that it can stand up on its own, ready for take-off! Once you have mastered the Rocket Base, you are ready to fold and launch your own rocket – or maybe a whole fleet of spaceships!

YOU WILL NEED
Square of metallic paper,
21 x 21cm (8¼ x 8¼in)

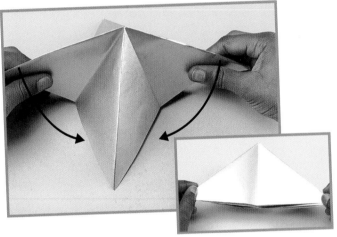

1 First make the Rocket Base as shown on page 11. Make sure that the shiny side of the paper is on the outside when you make your diagonal folds and on the inside when you make the horizontal folds. Hold the edges of a diagonal mountain fold and bring your hands in to make the triangle shape shown, with two flaps on each side.

2 Fold the outer edges in to the middle as shown. Turn the paper over and repeat.

3 Fold the outer corners to the middle. Turn the paper over and repeat on the other side.

 4

Fold the bottom points out at an angle as shown.

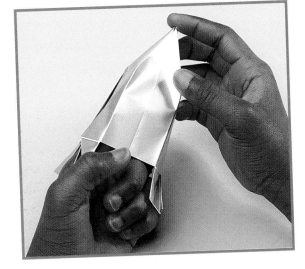

 5

Turn over and repeat.

 6 Carefully open up the rocket by placing your finger inside.

FURTHER IDEAS

Leave the rocket flat as in step 5 and glue it on to a greetings card.

Flapping Bird

This bird is a variation of the traditional origami crane, a bird that is a Japanese symbol for peace. The crane is also the symbol for many international origami societies. This version is simpler, but if you hold it in the right place, it actually flaps its wings. Once you have got the hang of the Bird Base shown on pages 10–11, you will be ready to fold this impressive project to amaze all your friends.

YOU WILL NEED
Square piece of paper,
24.5cm² (9¾in²)

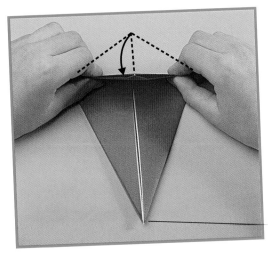

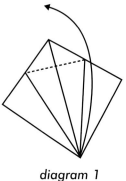

diagram 1

— open end

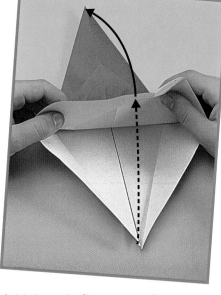

1 Start with the Bird Base, with the open end at the bottom. Fold the smaller triangle down, crease and fold back to its original position.

2 Unfold the side flaps as in diagram 1. Fold the bottom point up, covering the small triangle from step 1. Fold the point right up to the top, reversing the diagonal folds to form a diamond. Turn over and repeat this step on the back to make the shape shown in diagram 2.

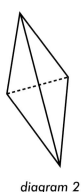

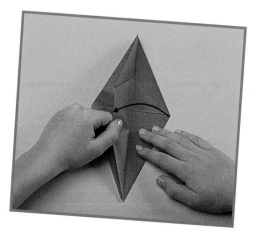

diagram 2

3

Fold the top flap on the right over to the left. Turn the paper over and repeat, folding the top right flap only to the left.

28

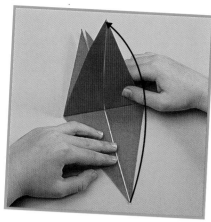

4 Fold the bottom flap up. Turn over and repeat.

5 Pull the hidden points in the middle out and down, and crease them in the position shown. These will make the bird's head and tail.

6 Fold the head down as shown, unfold it then make an internal reverse fold as shown at the top of page 9. To make your bird flap its wings, hold the two bottom points and gently pull them apart.

FURTHER IDEAS

Make birds in different sizes and colours, attach thread to their bodies and hang them from a coat hanger to make a mobile.

Blow-up Box

This classic Japanese origami design just looks like an interesting shape when you have finished folding it. However, if you blow into it, it inflates to make a three-dimensional box. Fold the Rocket Base first, and with a few simple folds and some clever tucks, you will soon have an origami shape with a built-in surprise!

YOU WILL NEED
Square piece of paper
20 x 20cm (8 x 8in)

1 Begin with the Rocket Base. Fold the bottom corners of the two front flaps up to the top point.

2 Turn the paper over and repeat on the other side.

3 Bring the two outer corners of the front flaps in to the centre and crease as shown.

4

Turn the paper over and repeat.

5

Make sure the loose points are at the top and tuck the front two loose points in the triangle pockets as far as you can. They will not go all the way in. Turn the paper over and repeat.

Top

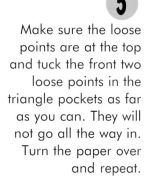

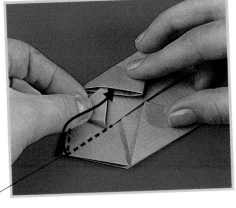

6

Hold the paper lightly between your fingers and thumbs. Put the open end to your mouth and blow into the opening. The box should now inflate.

FURTHER IDEAS

Make boxes in bright metallic colours and hang them up as Christmas decorations, or make red lanterns for Chinese New Year.

Index